The Pitch
is on the Way

Poems About Baseball and Life

by Dan Liberthson

Illustrated by Nicolette Ausschnitt

Printed by Daniel Liberthson, San Francisco, CA 2008

"Catcher" and "The Mound" first appeared in *Elysian Fields Quarterly* (2002)

"Flying Catch," "Spring," "Bench Player," "Catch," "End of the Slump," "Baseball at Seven," "Power," and "Hall of Fame" first appeared in *Spitball: The Literary Baseball Magazine* (2004-6)

Cover and interior illustrations by Nicolette Ausschnitt

Cover design and layout by Joe Bui Art Direction and Fish Tank Maintenance

ISBN-10: 0-9787683-1-0
ISBN-13: 978-0-9787683-1-7

To obtain additional copies of this book by mail, see website **Liberthson.com** or send $16.95 per copy (includes tax, media rate postage, and handling) by check or money order payable to Daniel Liberthson to:

Dan Liberthson
P.O. Box 31581
San Francisco, CA 94131-0581

Printed in the U.S.A.

Acknowledgments

My deepest gratitude to Kathy Rawlins, my wife, fellow fan, and first reader; to my writers group, in particular Judy Windt, who though relatively innocent of baseball edited my initial stabs at these poems; to my baseball buddies, Joanne Whitney, Paul Courter, and Jeff Hammond, whose saavy (I hope) kept me from embarrassing myself too badly; to Nancy Faass, for excellent editorial suggestions; to Nikki Ausschnitt, a terrific artist; to Joe Bui, friend and cover designer; to Nancy Etchemendy, Nancy Peterson, Eric Radzwill, and Bob Rose for helping with the all-important connections; to Brian Doyle for his encouragement; and finally, to Peter Magowan for his enthusiasm, and to him and the San Francisco Giants organization for their lovely new stadium, where many of these poems were born.

Contents

Part Three: The Scene, the Fans, the Seasons

Foreword
by Peter Magowan

Anyone who knows and loves baseball will enjoy this remarkable collection of poems by Dan Liberthson. They remind me so much of my own passion for the game, which started when I first began to play and watch as a little boy. Dan's poem "Catch," for example, brought back memories of endless games of catch with my friends—games we loved so much that we couldn't bear to stop until it was too dark to see.

Among the poems about each fielding position, "The Left Fielder and the Wall" reminds me of all the times I risked my neck climbing a brick wall for balls hit over my head—all that mattered was making the grab. Home runs were saved by my miraculous catches, and by the spirits of Willie Mays and Joe DiMaggio, who helped me to such heights. And what about all the trees I ran into trying to corral a long drive? I loved the game so much it hurt them more than it hurt me.

Dan captures all that and more in his portraits—from how beautiful and difficult the game is to how much both players and spectators can be surprised, delighted, and frustrated by any particular action on the field. From the first poem to the very last, I could not put this book down. I was happy and sometimes sad, but always engrossed. And I learned some things too—about baseball and poetry and how they can both relate to real life.

In "Second Baseman," for instance, Dan compares the second bagger to a merchant who "must ply both sides, steady middleman who takes what's offered on the right, parlays it to his cohort on the left." In an instant, that analogy brought to mind my 25-year career as a merchant at Safeway, and how the skills I needed then apply to the game of baseball. And in poems like "Past Present" and "A Fan," Dan explores the remarkable capacity of baseball to pick people up when they fall, to give them the grit to go at it for another season even when the chips are down.

I recommend *The Pitch is on the Way* to anybody who believes, as I do, that life is so much better when baseball is part of it.

Peter A. Magowan
President and Managing General Partner
San Francisco Giants

Author's Note

Baseball has meant a lot to me. So when I sit down to write poetry, which is based on my strongest impressions of and encounters with life, I often write about the game. Baseball has molded my preferences, my thoughts, and my approach to living as much as any other single experience. This book of poems is my tribute to a game that is embedded not only in American life but in the lives of many peoples throughout the world.

During my childhood, even with only a Minor League home team, the Rochester Red Wings, baseball became my secret world, a magical shelter from all abrasions on the way to adulthood. Still, I yearned for a Major League team. When I finally grew up and moved to San Francisco in the late 1970s, Candlestick Park and the Giants became my enchanted world of retreat and release, just as radio and TV games, baseball cards, and baseball talk with my friends had been when I was a kid.

In recent years, the brilliantly designed ballpark that the Giants built on the San Francisco Bay, with views to the water and the hills beyond, has replaced Candlestick as my summer Mecca. Sitting among the seagulls and sparrows in the sharp, clear air and watching ships negotiate San Francisco Bay bring my imagination to life. The stories and heroes, the players, the play itself, and the history of baseball have all made their way into poems conceived in the upper deck of that ballpark. The best views are behind home plate, gazing out at the Giants holding their own with bright fielding and sharp shots off the close-in right-field wall, or over it and into the Bay. In this park, you can sense the fog sniffing around the western wall of the stadium, hear the wind rattling the topmost tarps and see the flags fighting to get free. But inside, all is serene, the rude elements of the San Francisco summer climate that made Candlestick a survival contest are fended off as if by a charmed circle.

Perhaps the same charm makes this ballpark so nurturing of the poetic imagination. Many poems in this book are full of the details of baseball, the joys and perils of each position, the fabled history, the skills, rhythm, and language on display as the game unfolds. Other poems explore the game as a metaphor of living, a reflection of my strongest experiences and those of fans across the world. Because baseball has so deeply woven itself into the fabric of my life, I feel that I want to give the game and those who love it some record, some celebration of the pleasure and sustenance it has given me. So, thanks for tuning in, all you ball fans, you lovers of poetry, and you who simply want to be entertained. Hold onto your hats now, because the pitch is on the way.

Dan Liberthson, March 2008

Part One

The Game, the Kids,

the Heroes

The Game

I drove alone in grassy dusk
through north Ohio woods
where foreshadowings of color
crisped the leading edges of the leaves
and a deep chill curled in wait
for shorter, dimmer days.

A white-lit baseball diamond shone
a moment through fast condensing dark,
passing just as a batter connected
and I saw players circle the paths home
certain of their way,
safe within the game's design.

The ball was nowhere visible at first,
then rose higher so the light
reflected from its white as from a facet.
Heads turned toward its flight
above the circling moths and hopeful swifts,
beyond the fence and down into the gloom.

Through the tilting years since,
the fat crack of that bat has filled me
with liquid memory, preserved the game
in amber snapshots to play on, night or day,
be I present or away, darkly speeding body
circling the loop on hurtling Earth.

The Field

Within asphalt and then concrete rings,
shielded like an embryo in eggshell
lie a green field, blue sky, open air.
Drawn up and out, the fan floats above
the field: players jump, glide, catch,
swing, throw, incredibly gifted
jugglers nurtured by that fertile place,
as they were in centuries past,
nearly as free as the swallows that dip
and cross their own sustaining air.

Here, in this protected openness, life
so breathing full plays heedless of loss
or win, moving and moved for pure joy.
Every woman, his and theirs, is beautiful,
and the men in their intense adoring
and children rapt in their lost worlds.
Nothing matters, not his sad dead cat,
all too alive psychotic sister,
bitter mother, ironfaced father,
soulsucking job, waiting:
it's gone, dissolved and washed away.

Clean, untouched by misfortune,
he follows the ball's wake toward freedom
and finds it, safe and round and fat
at the apex of the arc, moment of complete
suspension before gravity wins and the ground
rushes up to claim, grip, surround.

So many bright moments flash by
before the crowd heaves a final sigh,
seeps down the aisles and drains away,
floating him like flotsam
through the opening gates to spill out
new-hatched into the same gray world.

Already he can scarcely recall
how it felt to be so briefly free:
ah, but it was beautiful, and must live on
somewhere, waiting to return—perhaps
in a cell or two behind the seeking eye
of that Heermann's gull flying seaward.

The Moment

Hitter may stretch, twitch,
fiddle with gloves, hitch his belt
and dig dirt like a marking dog,
but as the moment nears,
warm-up done,
he stills, ready to be
the heart of a whirlwind
driving the fat of the bat
along an instantly figured arc
toward a ball spinning past
so fast he sees only where it was,
yet slowed in mind to show
each curved seam turning.

Pitcher may shift his cap
palm the rosin bag, reglove,
kick at a clot, playing cat,
then start his wind-up fast,
but as the moment nears
he slows, potential energy
ready to become kinetic,
the heart of a whirlwind
driving toward the catcher's glove
so fast he never sees the seams
yet stilled in mind to show
the pressures round each lace,
how they sum to send the ball
where it should go.

Baseball at Seven

Sweet the smells of green grass,
oiled mitt lace I chew,
raw right earth that flings
my wondrous body over the field,
light and fluid as ever I'll be,
skimming, speeding, near to flight,
drawn by secret forces
to the white ball that slinks through dusk,
canny as a feral cat
crazy afraid of my pocket and web—
sooner the snarling world than be caught—
but, chased down and stalked to ground
step by seeking step, snared at last
in my mitt stashed in my drawer,
snug inside, hide hidden in hide—
never, however long the search,
abandoned on the open field
to the black teeth of night.

Names

So much power is in dead men's names:
Mathewson, Hornsby, Wagner, Ruth,
speak more vibrantly than any living.
We've forgotten how to remember now,
but then, a baseball card could bring to life
a man, a team, a season, play by play.

Bright spirits step out of a past
luminous beyond our dried-up time,
an age when life happened only once,
could not be copied and replayed,
took root in memory and grew
bigger, deeper, fresher there, like seeds.

Bench Player

It's long past bedtime
but that's half the delight—
tented in my blanket,
crackling radio at my ear
as the Rochester Red Wings
(Minor League, but mine)
play the Triple-A World Series.

Shetrone, Powell, Valentine,
these names are spells to me,
conjure silhouettes alive
against the blanket's weave, powered
by streetlight rays and waves of applause
trapped in my transistor like ocean in a shell.

Clean-up hitter swings, and my blood
sings along the arc, rocking heart
pounding ribs as bat on ball cracks
and I leave my body to follow,
rise through the cool night,
evade opposing mitts and land
free and fair in the right-field grass.

Coming back, we rise like the red horse
that wings over trees and fields,
Pegasus, my dream mount, invincible
as long as I keep just the right pressure
on the radio speaker with my thumb:
too little or too much and the sound

smashes like a waterfall on rocks.
Out in the night the pitcher winds
and speeds the ball in, but my grip
bends its path, forces it to the bat:
mind power surges through my fingers
to shape the game the Red Wings' way.
Bottom of the ninth and the count is full,
hold your breath, think *home*, and *PRESS*.

Power

Rocco Colavito rolls like thunder
from my child tongue. That righteous name
alone paralyzes pitchers, but add the big bat
that ends warm-up swings pointing straight
at their heads like a shotgun muzzle
and how can they face you or ever get you out?
I have your pale ash bat, a stick of power,
thin of handle, swelling in the barrel stout
like a battle mace forged whitehot in flame,
your utterly sure signature curving on the face.
Rocco Colavito, I chant your name as I bat,
in my mind's grim silence, cherish the power
surging from the ground through my trunk
up that ravening club, but still flail
as the steelhard ball whistles past.

It's only just: with a name like mine
how dare I hope for power like yours?
I have no magic nor right to borrow any.
A tremble of tears skims my eyes till I remember:
you too swing at anything, wild axeman,
strike out far more than you connect, yet
you swing strong, and when you hit, it's gone.
I point my bat straight at the pitcher and grin.
Rocco Colavito, I whisper, and swing again.

The Breaks, Kid

Flames spark from the heels of the Fastest Boy on Earth.
He can catch anything, shallow or deep, right or left.
Special springs in his feet jump him high.
Magic glyphs inked on his glove lure the ball.
A dragon circles the thumb, a viper crosses the web.
Supersonic, he runs and dives for a fungo to short right,
skimming the grass belly-down like that snake.

Out, out he stretches, till his glove snaps up its prey.
"Way to hustle!" Coach yells, "d'you kids see that guy?"
The Fastest Boy balloons with pride until he floats away.
Up in the sky, he has no clue he'll never again rise so high.
Coach puts him at third next day, there to pass the season
grubbing grounders from the dirt, watching them squirt
between his legs, or throwing way wild over first base,
as if the ball sought a mate among those high flies he'd chased.

Child's Play

I play the World Series with marbles
on our vine-laced Persian carpet:
its palaces are bases,
its bowers become dugouts
where my heroes' cards wait
for their manager's hand.
I play both sides, home and away,
hitter and fielder—as always
no one on my team but me.

Adult shapes, fat and crooked,
bald and creased or worn thin,
edge around me,
pass through the house smiling
down as if to say dear child
you know nothing outside
your magic carpet, which
one day you'll find is only a rug
that will take you no place at all.

But I have just jumped
an impossible height, caught
Roger Maris' hot line drive to right
and brought it back over the fence.
The roar of the crowd
puts any doubt to rest:
in that moment I am blessed
and that moment is all there is.

Catch

(For Robert Teti, wherever he may be)

Age twelve in a suburb means tedium,
measured as by metronome strokes,
empty as the silence when they stop.

Arms swinging to and fro,
a hardball's weight slung high,
and carefully looped at one another
(*thock* on *thock*, the ball in our gloves),
serfs to Boredom, my best friend and I
pivot and cast in thick summer air,
with slow-motion care, dying
as we grow, not knowing what to do
but throw, count our throws,
and anoint ourselves secret heroes
as the totals mount day by day.

Five hundred caught without a miss,
a thousand till the ball slips out
and thuds on the pavement, heavy
with the weight of our entrapment,
and finally, one late-August day,
with rain bulging the fat sack of clouds
(as near to pouring as Fall was looming)
and pressing down every breath,
somnolent with high wet depth,
it seems we cannot miss for trying,
as if we pitch through water and float

over and over to our rainbow throws,
until we reach 2000 flung and caught,
a number so impossible we know
we'll never get there again, and then
simply stand and stare and wonder,
not knowing how to end, to miss
deliberately or go on and on and on,
the meaning of this waiting moment
sinking in, as if one gigantic emptiness
were ending, another, similarly huge,
about to begin.

We know we have done a thing
no one else would think to do
or value, so we keep it to ourselves
and, silent, watch each other glow.
Nothing is the same, nothing changed.
The rain bag breaks. The flood come,
we turn toward home and run.

Mitt

Ever since my first real mitt,
I've loved the smell of leather,
smell that is a feel,
so rich and thick it is,
skin of my best living.

Warren Spahn model,
neatsfoot oil darkened,
Rawlings Trap-eze TJ7
stamped circled on the pocket,
Made in U.S.A. across the heel.

17

These words were totemic,
like Broadway's bright lights,
affirming hidden order, higher power
acted on my behalf, like incantations
making all possible things certain.

When I wore my mitt
I changed, like Clark Kent,
into a thing more potent
than a spindly boy—a being
imbued with Spahnie essence.

This claw glove that grappled
a baseball snug to its pocket
now has been flattened
by the slugfat softballs
of later, heavier years.

Artifact of an age when catches
were made with both hands
at penalty of coach's scolding,
it was born before mitts mutated
into monster gloves big as fishnets—

but no matter, that's irrelevant now.
The smell of leather lately
visits me only in shops.
Days when it mixed with slid grass
come only in dreams.

Hall of Fame

In the Hall of Fame the winners pose,
strutting past on full parade:
three-fingered Mordecai, Hornsby,
Ruth in his glory, Cobb in his fine shame.

Stuck up poster-high they flaunt and glitter,
heroes bright and bronzed, above the rest,
who at one sight can bring a childhood back,
tempting with a simpler time, a ball, a bat.

But what of the faces they stepped on,
bases spiked on their path, skin scored,
skulls cracked, blocked hard and down
swinging, faces gone out of the show?

Men like Piersall, maddened by the game,
and the silent ones who played the bitch in pain?
In another heroes' hall, Heorot of Hrothgar's fame,
Beowulf loved the unnamed men Grendel maimed.

Comrades lost, for battle-glory killed or lamed,
Baseball's Hall has missed though the Game
echoes with their pain: this Hall's unfinished when angels
play men—lacking frailty, they cannot win our love again.

Even in baseball heroes' stories (forget ordinary thanes),
some verity is missing, obscured by the veil of fame:
as if, for Beowulf, that final dragon never came
to try his spirit's temper, the truth of his life's game.

As if he never fought too fixed on treasure,
so failed the perfect measure of immortality
by cleaving to a precious thing and forgetting
precious souls—by narrowing as he grew old.

Cobb paranoid with bourbon, Mantle debauched again,
Shoeless Joe bribed, Rose in the gambler's den,
these stories skimped dilute their heroes' hold—
they'll be loved as fully human only fully told.

Ted Williams

Eyes sharp as a raptor's,
hands quick as talons,
he'd swing with such precision,
the ball screamed to rest.

Yet he grew monumental
only when he laid down bat
and talent, opened his eyes full
and began to love his enemies.

Old Diz

I was so young
when they yanked Dizzy Dean off TV
(for being the most colorful commentator
ever, because that might corrupt
the English of innocents like me),
it was the first and worst betrayal:
so bad that when we got color TV
it seemed less colorful
than black and white
though Pee Wee did his best
without Dizzy's red-clay Alabama drawl.

I try to remember the wild ride
of Dizzy's words, slang far spicier than
the bland standard English that sops
our airwaves and silts our minds.
Forty years later, I need to revive him,
to retrieve the tang of real language.
His voice surfaces and merges with mine
to broadcast for our fans a dream play
that is, though it never was.

"On a hard drive into the gap he's
off to the races, rounds first like a mare
with a stud horse on her tail and
no! He got spiked when he slud
into second, and you bet that ham'll
be swole up like snakebite tomorrow,
hurt more'n a weevil chewin' your cotton—
but he's gonna stay in there and play the game.
Ladies and gents, you gotta admire that man."

Past Present

In 1968, a year of acid despair,
I sit in a blue Chevy II
beside a sandlot diamond
watching kids play, eating
a 16-ounce, 75¢ can of salmon,
college sophomore flunking out,
stewing in a broth of pain.

I eat with my fingers, no bread or
drink, eat for mere survival,
all pleasure lost. The soft vertebral
bones condense between my teeth.
My head is one of those bones,
compressed by giant molars.

From a field shot with spring green
come the rising whoops and falling groans
of boys swinging, sliding, winning, losing.
At precisely the moment I imagine
the quickest way to be rid of myself,
the ball evades the catcher, finds a hole
in the backstop and rolls to my car.

He ditches mask and glove,
ducks behind the screen,
and as he bends to get the ball
finds my eyes through the windshield.
Rising, he samples my gaze again, intense
as a man's just blinded, frantic to see.

He is short, brown, round-faced.
Big dark-lashed eyes shine as he
flashes a grinful of teeth,
waves, theatrically spins, and runs off.
Black and compressed as a briquette, I still
can't help but smile at his retreating back,
a smile that lingers and will not die.

Long after the game ends
and the kids walk home tossing their mitts
high in the cooling air,
I stay. Something has changed.

When the sun starts down
I drive away, knowing
that whatever happens I will live
till a time decades on, when some free
unimaginable me will taste this day:
pink salty juice in my mouth, warm sunlight,
green leaves, the ball, the boy, the smile.

Part Two

The Players

and the Plays

The Mound

On this high place everything begins:
energy concentrates and strikes,
guided by craft through the air,
to scorch, freeze, or deceive.

The pitcher shapes this world
in his grip, remakes it every play,
priest while his strength lasts,
sacrifice when finally it fails.

I have been king of that hill,
felt my blood hum and swell,
then flow from wounds
beaten in by my own mind:

the lash of will laid across
my stubborn treacherous body
only cutting channels for tears
to follow, from the pure shame

a child alone can feel in failing.
Now I play other games
but still feel the echo of that pain
when a yanked pitcher hits the dugout.

Beyond comfort, he sits in misery's grip
huddling in his cave of disgrace
reliving disaster foaming in again,
as waves, one by one, bite off a beach.

Yet even in this back room of despair,
with ghosts of childhood tears crawling
down his face, he knows he'll climb
the mound again and start another game,

prays some god's favor that this time
he'll rise and set their bats to rest,
impose control and hold it till he wins
and lives in sunlight—this time, or the next.

Catcher

Senior warrior, counselor,
he crouches at the still center,
then sets the world spinning
with the minutest sign:
the diamond breaks light
into prismatic motion,
and all the game's colors
bloom from his glove.

Bat smolders orange with energy
sucked from the earth through
the hitter's tensile trunk and arms,
then flares red ripping
to meet the icehard ball
that dips, dense blue,
curves, elusive green,
waits, slow rust dream, or
melts whitehot with speed.

He sets all this in motion,
sits back and watches
for an endless moment, until
bat cracks ball, time begins,
the play explodes and then,
like every other player
on that field of chance—no!
more naked than any other
despite the armor he wears,
shorn of all his powers save
the flesh of his sacrificial body,
he stands like a wooden idol
blocking the path of the force
he has let loose:
unbroken light lancing around
the diamond, burning home.

First Baseman's Marriage

I always know where you are, love,
even with my back turned, the length
of me split wide on the path, torn
by that other woman, demon ball,

taunting just beyond my mitt.
I always yearn to get back to you,
my fetter and my freedom, even
when the bad hop leads me

sprawling into betrayal.
I want to come back, my love
before others take my place:
cocksure lead-offs flying up the line,

base thieves caught off guard
and diving back, bunt artists
burning up the path between
home, where they should stay,

and you—where they should stay away.
I'll trust you with another man only
if he's family—pitcher covering, or coach—
but I'll do anything to keep you

out of others' reach. Plump white
at the edge of the field, where fair
becomes foul and foul fair, you are
everything to me, my love. Always

I will make sure no one but me
gets to first base, no one makes so free.
If only my right arm were ten feet long
I could keep you from them all,

but lacking that, I'll stretch in pain,
guard you in a whirl of nerves,
face down the racing runner
hurtling toward your charms.

I'll do that, but I prefer the slow
moments we two dance alone:
when I pick the groundball clean
and come to you in perfect peace.

Second Baseman

If anyone plays the role of merchant,
it is he: not divine but necessary, he
must ply both sides, steady middle-man
who takes what's offered on the right,
parlays it to his cohort on the left, and so
connects the social fabric by his play.

Yet oddly this most practical of souls,
daily dealing in stuff bought and sold,
spurred by the goad of upturned spikes
on a runner hellbent for his teammate's safety,
lifts himself on high, become a spiritual man,
flying without wings to clear that human knife.
Floating in that moment, immortally aloft,
he takes the feed and spins to throw again,
watches the ball to the mark and then,
double-play down, resumes, earthbound,
his usual role of shopworn broker,
sharp eye out for the next exchange.

Third Baseman's Nightmare

In the hot corner, he floats quick
on the pads of his feet and waits
for the angry ball to chew his way,
aiming to cut off his ankles or spit
itself into his face with disdain.
Right-hander rips an inside fastball,
but the frozen third baseman can only
nurse his horror as ball eats through air,
impossibly slow screamer, looming,

growing harder and meaner, seeking
his soft parts like a mad dog—
knows he cannot duck or dodge
but must throw himself as hard
at his attacker as it rakes at him,
before it tears through and out
and he is whipped, gone.

Then he remembers who he is:
magician, acrobat riding on the wire,
gifted with the range of an eagle,
the swiftness of a hunting cat.
He'll not allow it: to be eaten up,
lanced and mocked, spun down
by any ball off any bat. He leaps
and takes the bad hop, pouncing
on the bounding prey, then,
airborne, frees from his web
the snuffed ball, winds and twists,
borrowing the hit's own thrust,
and throws with no waste motion
a strike that nips the runner by a toe.

Now he wakes, sweaty and blinking,
rubs his stubbled face, and mutters
why in the hell do I play third base?

Shortstop (the Texas Leaguer)

He's like a fiddler crab,
a being distilled fiercely frontward,
attention honed side to side,
so bravely wary behind his small
mobile wall of will that he allows
no doubt any attack could ever breach
the stretch of sand he claims
and gleans with glossy claw.

But he has not counted on
the high sky and the green sea
behind his indefensible back.
When threat bred there bears down
he turns and flees, beyond all certainty,
swivels frantically around his feet,
whirls his catch-claw everywhere.

Now forty thousand eyes watch
as falling from the sun, desolation grows:
though rocked in a surf of crowd sound,
that white descending silence
is all he knows.

The Left Fielder and the Wall

1

As a boy told Space was forever,
frightened, I imagined its end—
encircling wall thickening eternally:
beyond, no space but only more wall,
more density to ungape emptiness.

Now, grown, I miss endlessness,
space to run and make the catch
choked off by this ungiving Wall,
megalith that compels
acceptance of limit, loss, the end of play.

End of talent and desire,
barrier that always says no,
beyond here you cannot go,
brick, plank, or padded chain
your meaning is I am contained.

2

The nerves in my back feel you
waiting beyond the stunned space
between us, wallness threatening
as through some chemical message,
always imminent however distant.

Dreaming, I've walked your length
touching each sunwarmed place,
face and ear flush, to hear the stories
of shadows crushed within your space,
lives long past, watched, absorbed.

Game nights, after the crowd goes,
I walk your flank again to test
how the ball recoils from each crevasse,
spent, like a dull harpoon dropping
from a whale's hide in moonlight.

3

Sometimes you help me out,
give the ball back just in time
to cut a runner down at third
or hit the waiting relay man
who nails the leading run at home.

More often you take away—
squirt back the ball unplayably
or loom up high to block my chase
and crush with a hard embrace
my body's rising, my soul's hope.

You hold me closer than a wife,
harder than my father ever did:
I'd pray to you if I could hope,
pray anyway as I stand and watch
balls fly beyond you, disappear.

Shapeshifter of the Diamond

Center fielder, cock of the walk,
your glove is an agile beak, still now
but ready to snatch baseballs from the sky
as casually as breadrolls from a table.

I watch you glide across the field, half-bird,
touching ground briefly only from concern
some mortal might realize between plays
you are not one of us, alien ballherd.

Gravity is gravy to you, just fuel to burn
running up walls, as Chinese martial artists,
gifted with catapult legs, duel in midair,
above rooftops never rattled by baseballs.

I've seen you reach a talon past the wall
and snatch your team's life back,
as when a medic re-ignites a blown-out heart,
coaxing it back from past the final fence.

You catch the ricochet barehanded,
cut down the runner sliding into second
with a peg as quick and targeted as a knife-
thrower's sure fling at a lovely spinning lady.

Coursing from the green bend of deep center
you slide under a pop fly
like a seal beneath a beach ball, then
spring to your feet in the same motion,

and briefly doff your cap in afterthought,
as if to say, I can't help it, it's what I am.
How does it feel to be a miracle, flying man—
is there anything, lucky one, you cannot do?

Right Fielder Mourning

First comes the crack.
Then, rising, the white arc.
In right field the big man
wakes from patience
to a dream going sour.

Feeling rooted as a tree,
he tears his legs free,
turns, drives them into stride,
stretches out his arm
in a prayer, then in despair
waves goodbye to the
fierce liner lasering
toward the glee
on the home fans' faces.

He'd like to metamorphose
into some trampolining
hotdog centerfielder capable
of leaping six feet and un-
stuffing the fruit
from the waiting maw,
but he remains himself.

Something stalks him,
large, dark, rank,
snarling for meat—
he has known it before
but managed to forget,

knows it now only when
the drive slams into the seats
with a hard and final sound—
the Beast of Defeat.

It swallows him in one gulp
made smooth by the profound
droop of his broad shoulders
as he takes the long trudge
back home.

DH

Apparition
embodied only to bat,
otherwise nonexistent
like a spirit confined
to the space above its grave
or a vampire viable only at night,
recognized by only half the world
I lead even less than half a life,
materializing four or five times a game.
So insubstantial have I become
they seldom bother
to spell out my non-position.

One league believes me a figment
of the other's imagination,
an aberration for the most part
chained to the dugout floor
like a guard dog to its kennel door.
The other league summoned me
to this place where I will never taste
the freedom of the outfield grass,
the space beyond the dirt basepaths,
this place where like an addict I
swing only for the momentary high:
the crack, the run, the slide, done.

Hitter's Hunch

He plays the possibilities,
never tips his hand, and
gambling with a poker face,
swings where his best guess
suggests the ball may come
based on what he's seen
this very pitcher throw
today and many games ago,
on the fielders' shifts,
the pitch count and the weather,
the grass, cut long or short,
the runner, slow or fast,
some signal that's been passed
and things he cannot know,
like what the pitcher thinks he wants
or wants for him to think he wants to throw.
This infinite regression
has endless possibilities
for missing
and yet, never forget,
he still may connect.

Pinch Hitter

In a pinch they tell me
go in and take a swing,
there's runners at the corners—
you might just hit that thing.

Stay cool and pick your pitch,
don't hack at all he brings:
we're only three runs down
and you could tie this game.

Don't swing for the fences,
this guy's a sinker man—
you'll only end up topping it
straight back into his hand.

For twelve years playing in the league
I've watched this pitcher ride
his curveball round the corner
with a swoop and then a glide.

And when he's got his fastball,
it runs up sharp and in
and makes you bail for Sunday
to save a busted chin.

You know he thinks you're thinking
last time he worked you in
so he knows you're looking outside
and might come in again.

He grins to show his shark teeth
and goes into the stretch,
checks the runner back to first,
and brings it to his chest.

With leg kick high, his motion flaps,
the wind-up gives no clue
what sort of chop or suey
he might serve up to you.

Streeek one! the umpire bellows
as a screwball nicks the plate.
Streeek two comes even quicker,
a fastball—I swing late.

I work him for a foul or two
in between some balls—
nearly bite on one of them
but get a lucky call.

The payoff pitch is on the way,
I watch the seams rotate:
is this high heat, a cutter,
or a slider breaking late?

There's nothing left to do
but swing and go for broke.
I may come out a hero,
I may end up a goat.

A regular in the line-up
gets five at-bats a game
while I get maybe one in five
and a week of glory, or of pain.

Coach

Some try so hard to fly they
flame out from pure friction
and screech down to the Minors
trailing smoke in a dead spin
and though I know they will go
it's hell to watch it happen.

Others are so damned cocksure
no one can teach them anything,
least of all an old Methusaleh
who won't jive and offers no bonus.
They will bounce around,
up and down, maybe learn
to make it in the end or maybe not:
by then, no one will care but them.

Some soak in everything
like deep quiet pools.
These I can read and shape
from inside before they know it
and they're the only ones
I come to love as my own sons.
But they too drift off where the current
of their talent takes them.

At last I hover at the sideline,
passing them signs but no longer able
to read or sway their minds.
They will do what their hairtrigger
nerves tell them to, make the right
or the wrong choice before I can
signal or they begin to think.

When they win, some part of me
will lose, for they'll never hear me,
out here on the edge of time,
above the din of their young joy.
And when they lose, I will win
because I'll be back in their hearts,
their comfort once again.

Manager

If we don't grab the brass ring this time,
no more passes on the big carousel.
It's what they call a parting of the ways.
Ownership will politely (or not) say
Johnny, we love you, but you took
that great bunch of guys we bought
and blew it for the last season.
You're big with the promises
but come delivery time you choke.
It's the money, stupid, our money.
So nothing personal but now
you and yours check out.

Never mind that it worked
in another town in another time:
no hard-luck story, no past glory
means a thing once the chime
of coin hitting the till goes quiet,
the turnstyles still.
Fans won't come if you don't win
and you won't win if they don't come:
these are facts you can't run from.

So shaking hands means nothing now
but goodbye.

Batboy

When I grow up
I want to be just like them.
I don't care if they lose
though I'd rather be
them when they win.

Ump

The worst is when I know
I'm wrong
but can't admit it
or the next time
they'd know I'm not
immortal
and tear me to pieces.

They come at me like Job
wild with righteous fury,
begging for the true,
the holy call
and if only they knew
how much I'd like to say
yes, you're right
and take the hurt away—
I called it as I saw it
but I saw it wrong.

Just once to get to say
it's not your fault
it's not mine
I really can't see everything
all of the time:
how else could those
bad things happen?

Yes, dammit, they just happen.
Get over it.

Play ball!

Groundskeeper

Your standard Kansas sodbuster
wearing out my ass on the hard prairie
I would have been
save for the grace of this game.
The field is a sacred grove,
every blade of grass a holy tree.
And let me tell you of the feet
that have kissed the ground I groom,
the feet of men whose footsteps
faded from this grass into history.

I've had a drink or two, as you can tell
but I'll still rake a furrow in these basepaths
curved as fine as any prima donna's breast
that ever graced the stage.
Ah, I could wish for nothing more
than the welling of this grassy scent
in the wide of my nose when I water
unless it be the moment toward gametime
when I stoop to put the batter's boxes in
without which the game could not begin.

It is my finest hour to place the frame
before the early crowd, the real fans who know
to come for practice and the humming morning air:
they appreciate the fine precision of my hammer taps
that knock the pipes to set the chalk lines out

and leave the double boxes where they make
the shape that guides the whole configuration
at the plate, sets the picture up before the pitch.
Then I sit invisible, watch what I have shaped,
and never show my face again until they leave the gate.

In the Beginning

He's like a boatman on land
but still encumbered by his craft,
strangely walking within its frame,
the hull perhaps devoured by dry rot.
His hands in rowing position do not move
but hold it up, balanced, careful, tender—
so the groundsman carries the template
for the batter's box and sets it down
precisely at home plate.

The sacred moment framed in space,
he shapes it now in time, with twin
hammer knocks on each rectangle side,
then lifts to display a perfect replica
of that original boat or window frame
outlined in chalk like a white shadow.

Late arrivals blunder among the rows,
interested more in beer and franks
than this poesis, boat become window
become stage for each aspiring batter,
who survives or falls, then departs
as in any other drama, to come again
or not.

Perhaps the crowd is right, this is no matter
in which to place faith or find comfort,
this limning of the sacred space where
all the play will start and end.
Maybe only the action matters—
for by mid-game the lines are smeared,
the forms broken, original shapes wracked
by the violence of succeeding moments,
sacred space substantially lost, except
to imagination, compelled to re-create it.

The Fan

View seat, upper deck.
From here I rule
and can command
everything to fit,
piece by puzzle piece,
though I cannot knit
from any perspective
my shredded outside life.

Dark gull shadows travel
across the grass: two
as the game starts, easily
tracked to their white templates,
but then more and more,
shadows attracting shadows
as blood attracts sharks
until so many wheel and wander,
it's impossible to tell which dark
is leashed to which white.
My gaze drifts away from the game,
the players' predictable motions.

Are these gull shadows,
changing like candleflame in wind,
elusive doors to other, better lands
blessed beyond any I have known
or the fenced game could show,
or to panic worlds disintegrating,
the work of sharks that knife below,

greedy for the human minds
on which they hope and prey?
Spinning through these opposites,
now the shadows black the field,
siphon this earth's light away
and lead me to pure vertigo,
toppling toward a skewed dimension
where only despair could live.

The crack of bat on ball
rescues me from headlong fall
to waiting symmetry,
and from a realm of loss
returns me to a game I understand,
a green and promised land
where all the pieces fit
and all the paths lead home.

Part Three

The Scene, the Fans,

the Seasons

Spring

Blood begins to press harder like
water swelling slightly just before the boil.
Limbs twitch for no reason and the heart,
always greedy for something special,
now wants something unnamable.

The smell of a leather shop intoxicates,
nostrils flare, snatch at grilled meat scents,
a riotous excitement spawns and grows
slowly at first, then with maddening lunges
like those of the rocking-horse winner
clinging to his silently plunging steed.
This morning I found myself swinging
the garden rake at a high outside acorn,
connecting above the trademark and sending
a vicious line drive up the middle—
caught by an outstretched branch!
I haven't been so giddy since I was seven.
Wound tight as thread around a baseball's core,
I can barely stop myself from screaming
for the whole street to hear—
Play ball!

Batter Up

The Romantic strides to the plate:
hands on the knob, pulling for the seats,
strike-out victim or home-run king
it's all or nothing when he swings.

The Cynic chokes up, closing his stance,
swings at nothing on the corners, only
solid possibilities—no wild rips for slams,
no passion when tight licks suffice.

The rare Enlightened One is calm
in every situation, never hurries
or hesitates, chooses his pitch:
expecting a hit, smiles at a miss.

Old Stoic in a slump takes his cuts,
good pitch or bad, with equal despair,
knowing he'll miss either way:
yesterday, today—its all a blur.

The Pessimist won't bother to swing:
crowds the plate in hopes he'll draw
the longed-for walk or get knocked
and trot without doing anything.

The Optimist flails at every pitch:
cocksure as a player can be
he thinks he'll hit whatever they bring
like a bird-dog chasing sparrows.

The Pragmatist hits it where they ain't:
bunts when they play back, butchers it
up the middle when they come in—
always gets the extra step.

The Believer thinks it's never over,
the Agnostic can't say if it is or not,
the Atheist thinks it'll be when it is,
the Nihilist thinks it is when it's not.

So we parade our temperaments
game after game, season upon season,
on pilgrimage to some finer place,
though where that is we cannot guess, or reason.

Wages of Sin

Fans gaze up in search of their places,
hold out tickets like divining rods,
hope and prayer painting their faces.

From someone else's seat,
I enjoy a view
much better than I bought
but suffer a penalty too
as more fans arrive
of unease incremental.
Stolen pleasure, sweet hurray!
Churning stomach, sour dismay.

Still more come:
the crowd closes in
filling seats perhaps at random
though I suspect
by some intent design.
Gazes scan and hesitate,
then pass on, as I imitate
a rightful owner propped
in my illicit space,
soon to be exposed, disgraced.
Sinner seeming righteous man,
don't you realize you're damned?

Yet the top of the fourth arrives
and no one's pressed a claim.
A surge of exaltation!
I'll get away with this transgression!

I should be whipping myself well,
birch to bare behind,
but I feel sunny and terrific
for the view is very fine.

Red Hot Here

It's the hottest day of the year.
I sit in my closed room
sweating and dreaming
of pools and breezes in fields,
this invention of coolness
a vaccine
to ward off meltdown,
saving me and the world
from pudding death.

One field is deepest green
intensifying beside beige sand
beneath white uniforms and glaring sun:
on it a bleached ball falls and rolls free
and the white and dark skins
reach easily from within their cloth,
flowing in smooth, crisp rhythms
over ever cooler grass.

There are two lights here,
lake-deep emerald and desert diamond.
Diamond cuts everything
you know,
scratches glass grooves steel
but rakes helpless on this green
that only grows deeper, floods,
cools everything to dream.

And He Gloves It!

Scorcher to the hot corner.
Third sacker reacts
like a roach:
peripheral nerves only—
no brain required.

The Wanderer

This stocky brown man,
broad and bony of face
who looks Tibetan or Nepalese
arrives at the top of field level
and peers down at the rows of seats
bewildered
after the long trail in,
as if his mountain slopes implausibly
have melted and re-formed
this staggered pyramid;
then collects himself, visibly
realizes all things are possible,
nothing absolute, and that he knows
where he is
no matter where he is:
climbs down with confidence,
bright-eyed yak herder
finding again his valley home
after seasons wandering the peaks.

Crowd Music

Late innings,
visitors at bat,
clean-up man due.
Relief staff gets
the pitch in true
but the big right-hander
pulls a long fly
deep to left, rising
into the blue.

The concert is conceived
in silence,
buoyed by held
collective breath,
crowd noise waiting
a whole rest,
while the composer ponders
paired possibilities:
breath expelled in flat relief,
descending triplet sigh
in minor key,
slurred as the ball
hooks, lands foul—
or if it stays fair
aching major scare
and a sharp trill
of despair.

The Winner

A few rows back from the left field line
sits a small boy with a glove, hoping with no hope.
The father looks at him tenderly, and sadly,
suspecting his child will spend a life
as he has done—on the sideline
waiting for a ball to come.
The mother, on the other side,
cradles his head with her palm.
He thinks of shaking it off,
to be ready if a chance comes, then slumps:
in the top of the ninth, he's tired, like everyone.

But at the bat's crack he strains forward,
half blind behind sweated glasses, wistfully
waving his black glove, like a dog's nose
sniffing for a morsel that's just not there.
The high liner twists foul and bounces
into the stands, where it ricochets, rattles,
trickles across an open seat, and falls
over the edge into the child's glove.

This once, at least, the ball has come to him.

Vendor

Get it here, get it here,
get your cold beer get
your peanuts cotton candy
sodas icecream Crackerjacks—

if you want it hard enough
and you got a couple bucks
you can get it here
or you can't get it anywhere.

But what do I get?

To sail a bag of nuts
over twelve seats and
nail the customer clean,
no runs, no errors, every time.

They cheer for me
whenever I play this trick
as much as for the guy who
catches the foul tip.

And what does that make me?

Vendor king, tracking four orders
at once, remembering everything
and pouring a beer balanced
on the short side of nothing.

Vendor slave hauling forty pounds
of sodas upstairs and down
without breaking sweat, counting on
one hand, making change with the other.

And what does that get me?

Once I counted every step
I climbed up or down in a night
at the old ball game and stopped
at a thousand, still rising.

I've seen faces smooth as silk
or rough as gravel
smile the same shining in victory,
droop the same dullness in defeat.

And does it make me happy?

You bet.

Appetites

From a hotdog, grilled green peppers tease.
    I want it.
Rattling Crackerjacks leap from their box.
    I want them.
Icecream sundae puffs in its plastic chalice.
    I want it.
Churros smell like beehives spinning past.
    I want them.
Cotton candy's siren song lures teeth to their doom.
    I want it.
In their yellow pool, nachos breast-stroke.
    I want them.
Foaming beer drenches my neighbor's throat.
    I want it.
Girls' bare backs gleam in the sun.
    I want them.

I want it all.

Pop-up splits second and third.
Shortstop yells

I've got it!

The Error of Their Ways

Trying too hard, that's error:
Fireballer over-throws,
lurches off the mound
as his pitch runs to the backstop.

Not trying hard enough, that's error:
catcher backhands a snake pitch
instead of jumping
for the body block.

Feeling too much pain, that's error:
aging first-baseman waves
a slow roller between his legs
past his knees' helpless shouts.

Haste (making waste), that's error:
second baseman turns his shortstop's throw
before he finds the seams; first sacker,
at the top of his leap, sees it sail away.

Taking what's not yours, that's error:
Third baseman flubs a shallow fly
by rights his left fielder's; then the rattled
rookie pitcher gophers a homerun ball.

Distraction, that's error:
bouncer kisses the shortstop's glove heel,
broken bat barrel flipping toward him;
E6, undeserved, but so it stays.

Dreaming, that's error:
left fielder gets a late start—
rising liner ticks his web
for double trouble.

Overconfidence, that's error:
center fielder lazily one-hands
the high fly ball that finds
a nonexistent hole in his glove.

Misjudgment, that's error:
right fielder overthrows his cut-off man
and suddenly the runner stands
safe at third, smiling.

So many ways to err
on so many days and nights!
it's amazing anyone
gets anything right.

Perfect Game

Like perfect love,
once in a lifetime.
Someone else's.

Got Those Ballpark Blues

Hitters get scythed by their own bats,
runners stumble as in gopher holes,
our line-drives slam into their mitts
like berry-drunk birds into window panes,
our clean-up man's entranced (streeek three!)
paralyzed like a bronze statue
by lust for a break-out slam,
and when we finally work a walk—
double-play, the purest cruelty, kills
hope just as it starts to grow, whacks
the sprouting dream before it fruits.

Our guy's two-strike pitches, low and
curved like beauty smiling open-lipped
are brutally murdered back up the middle.
Their foul tips skitter free,
ours buzz and die in the web.
Their pop-ups navigate beyond reach,
ours sail into gaping mitts.

The sun eats high flies and spews down
flaming meteorites to blind our fielders
who flail as if fending off vultures.
Umpires with the vision of rhinoceri
and every bit as ignorant and stubborn
charge around the field blowing calls
their way.

One of us must surely be a Jonah,
running from some sacred calling:
why else such misery? Find him,
throw him over! Trade the bum
and let him wreck some other team
or send him down until he lands
in a one-horse town
and never sees Double-A again.

Did someone hang his cap up backward,
open a gum pack from the wrong end,
lose the wad he chewed hitting that homerun
when his kid picked it off the headboard
and fed it to the schnauzer on the bed,
let his wife wash his lucky underwear,
forget to sign the cross before batting,
tie his shoes in the wrong sequence,
lose the only glove he's ever loved,
sit on the wrong side of the plane,
shave or not shave (either way we're screwed)?

Because dammit all there's got to be some reason
we've been stuck in this slump the whole season.

End of the Slump

One big long fat disaster, this season,
a slow-motion slog in the mud, as if
struck by sleeping sickness or malaria,
the ball devious as a drunk mosquito,
ducking under, twisting past, attacking
so I swung like a cripple in self-defense.

I was sitting on fastballs high and tight
up where I like, but swinging through them
like a tennis player with an unstrung racket.
When I thought curve, up came the screw.
I flailed like a blind man with a flyswatter,
couldn't connect with change for coffee.

So used to missing, when I jacked that sky-
deep fly off a three-two I just stood there,
like a kid whose girl says "let's not wait"
and peels off her blouse on the second date.
Coach kept screaming "run you fool"
till my legs took off by themselves.
Around first, seeing the ball slip down the wall
between their left fielder's legs, I cranked
into high, blew through second, tore after third,
slid headfirst, grabbed that plump white bag
like a guy who knows just what to do,
stood up proud, doffed my cap, and bowed.

Late September

Day game, midweek,
shank of the season,
home team sinking third,
visitors headed cellar-ward
and my slow season
passing too.

Attendance sparse
(pick a seat, put up your feet),
shrill whistlers rare,
cursing zealots gone,
and even the umps'
screw-ups mildly tolerated.
Neither fans nor players
have anything to prove.
Massive calm
between time's unleashed
glaciers.

Win or lose
doesn't matter, only
warm sun
blue sky
green grass.

Ball thwacks leather,
bat cracks ball,
players circle eternal.
I could stay forever,
finally coming home.

Flying Catch

Pounding flat out, I pursue.
The ball alone exists.
Angles close, distance shifts,
behind is only failure,
life's dispersing slick.

Diving, I fluoresce:
bird, soar and sail,
fish, skim wet grass—
snare the bait in my glove,
glide till the bright field
hugs me to its green breast.

Rolling, I stare into steel blue
autumn sky, smell burnt leaves.
Naked poplars at field's edge
glint in setting sun, licorice
crows rise raggedly, spiraling
where my kind cannot go.

Without doubt I know
at least I will have lived
when I die.

Sunday at the Park

(To Stephen Sondheim)

So vivid green, the field below, insistent
in the roaring sun: melding all our visions,
the big game takes our separate games
this liquid afternoon and fuses them in one.

Pointillist scene, the park condenses
from a swarm of discrete dots, static, yet
blending into a map of incipient motion,
as we disparate fans close to make a crowd.

Here's the wind-up, the pitch is on the way:
each attention fastens on the white spot of ball.
Not one of us knows what will happen next,
how the dots will rearrange, the possibilities

limitless even within the game: strike three,
a pop-up, wild pitch, home run, sacrifice of any
species, batter struck or pitcher battered—
and what about outside the game? One time

an earthquake came and made it all moot.
Some insist it's tedious, waiting for the pitch
time and time again, but these folks
miss the thrill each waiting moment

of their waiting lives contains: a fruit,
flavor forgotten but familiar, hung
once on time's tree—moment ripe for peeling,
glistening sections spread and savored,

tastes possible and actual sucked free.
Now another—can you reach it?—
on a higher, newer branch, slick with dew
condensed from your lifetime's passage.

The batter readies, crowd sound gathers in:
light rays through a lens project a world
printed on film and brought to life again,
but the reel is stuck, the pitch is still to come.

Impossible to believe that if we close our eyes
this technicolor mirage will remain, not the crackling
blank of film burned through, image flown in smoke.
Yet we all have faith the scene will start anew

the moment our collective wink's complete—
and this the miracle: eyes open again, everything
returns full strength; the film runs on, the batter
swings, gravity once more holds up and down.

It's like the birthday party when you were five:
close your eyes, guess the present,
but the gift is hidden, so far the lovely wrap is all.
The magician waves, and out pops the white rabbit.

Players and spectators all, eyes on the ball,
none knows what each pitch will bring:
such pleasure, such dread, anticipating!
Every moment of every day, the pitch is on the way.

About the Author

Dan Liberthson has a PhD in English literature from the State University of New York at Buffalo. Born in Rochester, New York, he has made his home in San Francisco and the Bay Area since 1978. Dan has published widely in poetry journals and also is the author of *A Family Album*, a book of poems that describes the joys and heartaches of growing up in a perfectionist Jewish immigrant family with a schizophrenic sister. For further information about Dan's poetry and to place orders for his books, please visit his website, **Liberthson.com**.

About the Artist

Nicolette Ausschnitt has an undergraduate degree from the Rhode Island School of Design and an MFA from the University of Michigan. Born and raised in New York City, she honed her drawing skills at a young age by sketching people on subways and buses on the way to school. For 15 years, Nikki participated in the San Francisco Open Studios. Her work is in numerous private collections and has been in many national exhibitions and competitions. She now lives in Yorkville, Mendocino County, California.

* * *

In the drawing on the following page, Nikki evokes the spirit of baseball in an image adapted from a mounted display by William Channing of Santa Fe, NM, in which 1940s era equipment is arranged in the posture of a catcher who has just taken the pitch. The deep tradition of baseball shines powerfully through timeworn catcher's gear that evokes pitch after pitch, catch after catch, down through the years.

But making the catch is never the final act: hauntingly empty, the mask demands to be filled. Accept its invitation! Step into the catcher's gear and come alive to the game's timeless excitement: what will the runners do, how will the play develop, what pitch will come next, and above all, what will happen now? This is the tantalizing mystery, the dynamism of the game and of our lives.

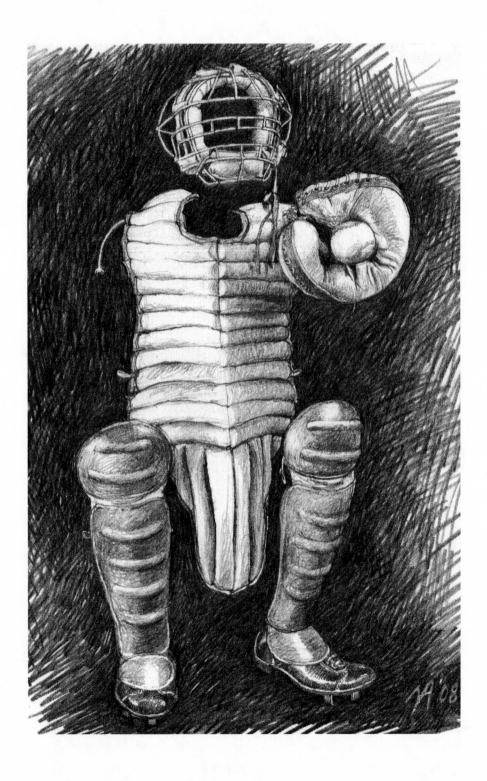